WHY THE SOUTHERN RULES ARE THE ULTIMATE RULES

"Surely we are all by now at least dimly aware that to catch a man, a woman must play hard to get. But there's more to it than that. Southern women have for generations conducted themselves by a code that allows us to pick and choose the man who is perfect for us and to control him (without his knowing it) for the rest of his life."

So begins *The Southern Rules,* the ADVANCED COURSE FOR WOMEN WHO ARE SERIOUS ABOUT TAMING THE MALE BEAST.

- Have you identified whether your man is Mama-Dependent or Mama-Deprived?

- Do you know how to strategize based on the nature of his mama-conflict?

- Have you identified his collegiate football team of choice and strategized accordingly?

- Do you know how to recognize a New-Age Southern Male (also known as a Wolf in Sheep's Clothing) and avoid him?

- Do you know when to cry and when not to?

- Do you know when to be soft, when to be hard, and when to learn to shoot?

If the answer to any of the above is "no," you need to read *The Southern Rules* before it's too late!

D1463047

THE
Southern
RULES

The Advanced Course for
Women Who Are Serious
About Taming the Male Beast

By Ellen Patrick

SWEET
WATER
PRESS

BIRMINGHAM, ALABAMA

This edition published for Sweetwater Press by arrangement with Crane Hill Publishers and Cliff Road Books.

ISBN 1-58173-232-5

Project development and management
   by Southern Lights Custom Publishing
Cover design by Matthew Dorning

Printed in the U.S.

10   9   8   7   6   5   4   3   2

Table of Contents

Helpful Checklists

THE
Southern
RULES

Chapter One

WHY THE SOUTHERN RULES?

Surely we are all by now at least dimly aware that to catch a man, a woman must play hard to get. But there's more to it than that. Southern women have for generations conducted themselves by a code that allows us to pick and choose the man who is perfect for us and to control him (without his knowing it) for the rest of his life.

The Southern Rules represent the advanced course for women who are truly serious about taming the male beast. They can be used by any woman, anywhere—on any man, anywhere. They were invented by women in the Southern United States, where men are exceptionally childish and unruly, for the purpose of creating and perpetuating a civilized society.

Be careful when using *The Southern Rules*. They are powerful medicine. They work. If you use them on the wrong man you'll be in trouble. You might get stuck with him. That is why it's important to understand and then carefully select your prey—a topic we'll explore in subsequent chapters.

But, you might first ask, if these rules are so well-known and used by Southern women, why must they be written down? The reason, for all of you who have been in a coma or a convent, or have been co-opted by feminism into behaving like common streetwalkers, is that—God forbid—even Southern society is now changing. The younger generations who are coming along, with their latchkey children, MTV addicts, and general counterculture trash, are in danger of losing their grip on *The Southern Rules.* This could spell the end of civilization as we know it. For, after all, if we lose the civilized South, we have lost the nation. Perhaps even the world. And we will have certainly lost ourselves.

Thus this little book is designed to keep intact our Southern code of dating and mating. Read it, use it, and you will happily remain forever in charge of that runny-nosed, mother-conflicted, big-talking, insecure but adorable Bubba in your life.

Chapter Two

REMEMBER SCARLETT AND KEEP HER HOLY

$\mathcal{K}$ind reader, it pains me to even have to write this chapter. To think that there could be one lone Southern woman out there who does not understand what is worth preserving forever in our leading archetype is, well, a dismal prophecy for us all.

Make fun of her if you will. Pooh-pooh her passions if you must prove you are intellectually above it all. But never forget that Scarlett always got every single thing she ever wanted. You might argue that she blew it in the end by turning into just the kind of bleary-eyed, mush-mouthed fool that men can't stand. This, you might argue, caused Rhett to turn away from her at last. But you know in your heart, don't you, that she gets him back eventually?

The lesson here is that even the Scarletts of the world have their moments of weakness and make mistakes. The lesson, in case you have had your head buried in the pawpaw patch, is that you can learn from Scarlett and avoid those mistakes. If the man of your dreams comes along, you want to be in a position to recognize him and strategize appropriately for a lifetime of wedded bliss. Don't, like Scarlett, go dreaming after some mewling mama's boy like Ashley (unless that's what you really want). Don't, when you finally figure out which man is the right one for you, don't ever EVER cry in front of him (except in certain highly tactical maneuvers—see Chapter Eighteen, "The Importance of Tears"). Never NEVER beg. Southern women don't have to beg because they have much more sophisticated ways of getting what they want.

What you should do is remember the basic strong points of Scarlett's character and incorporate them, in your own way, into yourself. The Scarlett Checklist on the next page will help you do just that.

The Scarlett Checklist

1. Always know very clearly what you want.

2. Never doubt that you can have exactly what you want.

3. Never doubt that you are the most tantalizing girl at the barbecue.

4. Remember that men aren't everything. For the most part, they're just someone to eat barbecue with.

5. Never listen to anyone who tells you that you can afford to skimp on your wardrobe, hair, or makeup.

6. Take time to prepare yourself for the day. Use fancy soaps and bath salts and perfumes and powders, and hum to yourself while dressing.

7. Never let anyone know how long you take to prepare yourself for the day.

8. Always have a million dates in your datebook—and even if you don't, act like you do.

9. Eat like a bird in public. No matter what they say to the contrary, men are confused and unsettled by women with hearty appetites.

10. If another woman gets in your way, don't hesitate to connive against her. (Just make sure you do it well.)

11. Speak softly and carry a small pistol.

12. In front of the mirror, practice saying in a light-hearted fashion: "Fiddle-dee-dee!" It will put you in the appropriate mood of carefree girlish abandon that Southern men find so attractive. (Warning: Avoid saying "fiddle-dee-dee" aloud in public as people might think you're crazy.)

Chapter Three

KNOW YOUR PREY (AND YOURSELF)

*B*efore you do that thing Southern women do so well— that is, torture men with longing and desire—be sure you have the appropriate prey in your sights.

We'll go into this in more detail in the next two chapters, but basically, there are two elemental types of Southern men: the Mama-Dependent and the Mama-Deprived. Of course there are endless variations of both types, but most men fall into one category or the other. This is important information for two reasons. First, you must identify your prey by type so you will know how to strategize his capture. And second, you must be clear about which type is right for you so you don't accidentally end up with the wrong man. This happens more often than any of us would like, hence the endless roster of divorces even in the South, formerly the World Capital of Wedded Bliss. But times change.

So know your prey and know yourself. Since the next two chapters will talk about your prey, let's talk about you now by looking at three essential types of Southern female.

Which category best describes you?

Are You a Melanie?

1. Do you enjoy taking care of people, the way Melanie took care of Ashley?

2. Is having a family one of your main goals in life?

3. Would you sacrifice your life for home and hearth?

4. Is a job or career secondary or irrelevant to you?

5. Do you like to cook—a lot?

6. Do you tend to be a follower rather than a leader?

7. Do your interests tend to be dictated by those around you?

8. Do your hobbies keep you in or revolve around the home?

9. Do you spend time or have the urge to spend time in good works for the benefit of the community?

10. Are you the type who gets a thrill out of showing unexpected kindness to strangers?

If you answered yes to seven or more of the questions above, you are the Melanie type and will be happiest with the Mama-Dependent Southern man.

Are You a Zelda?

1. **Are you moody and sometimes considered by others to be "difficult?"**

2. **Do you have a way of charming strangers with your whimsicality and ethereal nature?**

3. **Do you feel confined when you are forced to spend too much time at home?**

4. **Do you relish the idea of being out in the world, having lots of new experiences?**

5. **Have you had lots of boyfriends or have lots of men had crushes on you?**

6. **Are you a dreamer at heart?**

7. **Do you basically expect others to adapt themselves to your needs?**

8. **Do you tend to be rather undisciplined?**

9. **Are domestic skills not your strong suit?**

10. **Do you have an artistic or creative bent?**

If you answered yes to seven or more of the questions above, you are a Zelda and will be happiest with either a slightly Mama-Dependent Southern man or a very VERY toned-down version of the Mama-Deprived man.

Are You a Hillary?

1. Have you worked your fingers to the bone in your single-minded determination to get ahead?

2. Is your career all-important to you? Would you describe yourself as driven?

3. Is having a family of secondary or little importance to you?

4. Do you have little patience with the neediness of others?

5. Are you highly focused and goal-oriented?

6. Do you expect to be waited on from time to time?

7. Do you have a very busy life with little time for dating?

8. When you have a leisure moment, would you prefer to be home with a good book than out with a man you're not intensely interested in?

9. Do you have little interest in what people think of you? Do you find yourself impatient with the niceties of society?

10. Do you dislike talking on the phone?

If you answered yes to seven or more of the above questions, you are a Hillary and will be happiest with the Mama-Deprived man.

If you find you don't totally fit any one of the three categories above, don't worry. These are archetypes designed to get you thinking about what kind of man you need. If you're like most Southern women, you will have a lot of Melanie in you—because most of us Southern women are raised by our mamas to think we have to wait on a man hand and foot. But just because you were raised that way, don't think you have to be that way. Take a close look at yourself. Have you always rebelled against that sort of thing and hated the way men expect you to hold out a pan and catch their tobacco plug for them?

You don't have to, child. On the other hand, if you truly enjoy taking care of someone lock, stock, and barrel—go for it.

The point is, pick the kind of man you want and go after him. According to *The Southern Rules,* of course.

Chapter Four

THE MAMA
FACTOR

*A*s we have mentioned in the previous chapter, Southern men fall into two basic categories: the Mama-Dependent and the Mama-Deprived. I don't care how much they cover themselves up with big-boy macho talk or New-Age sensitivity, they are all the product of their mamas. I can't emphasize enough how important this is in picking your man and strategizing his capture. You MUST identify the nature of his mama-conflict.

There are two kinds of Southern male because there are two kinds of mamas. First, you have the mama who lays her life down for her children. She's your basic martyr who lives for her children, especially her boys, and cooks and cleans for them even when they are forty years old. She's the kind of mama who wipes their boogers and picks up their underwear behind them until the day she dies.

What this type of mama creates is the classic mama-smothered male—a man who expects you to wait on him just like his mama did. A man who, with the proper training, can be a hearty provider and healthy romantic partner, but who will always be to some degree on the childish side of maturity.

This is no great sin. Very few of us, male or female, ever

truly reach full maturity. And if you are a Melanie type who needs a man who needs lots of taking care of, this may be just the type of man for you.

But it is important that you recognize what kind of man you are dealing with under the surface, before you use *The Southern Rules* full strength on him. That way you won't find yourself stuck with the wrong kind of catch.

The handy checklists on the following pages will help you identify The Mama-Dependent Male and The Mama-Deprived Male.

The Mama-Dependent Male

1. Chews with his mouth open because his mama never had the heart to tell him not to.

2. Bites his fingernails and spits them across the room because his mama never had the heart to tell him not to.

3. Is as rigid as a baby in his routines, i.e. has absolute set times when he needs to eat or he turns ugly.

4. Has trouble in general rolling with the flow. Does not like ambiguity.

5. Needs time to stay out playing with his friends.

6. Has strong likes and dislikes in food and drink, i.e. your basic meat-and-potatoes man. Alcoholic beverage of choice: beer.

7. Has powerful regional loyalties to his town, his state, his school, and probably his favorite football team—also to his friends and family.

8. Is usually a hard worker. (Beware the mama's boy who can't seem to find his calling in life.)

9. **Always does what he says he will do. Has a strong belief in honor. Tends to be conservative in his political views but tolerant and kind to people as individuals.**

10. **Has strong pride in his masculinity. Does not cotton to artistic experiences or events such as the ballet, symphony, or art openings.**

Generally speaking, the Mama-Dependent Southern man, while fully capable of being obnoxious and even intolerable to the point of boorishness, has a certain basic niceness to him and a natural generosity that, with the proper encouragement, can blossom into a lifetime of tender love and caring. Depending on how mama-influenced he is, catching him can be as easy as shooting fish in a barrel.

Now let's take a look at the counterpart of our mama's boy, the Mama-Deprived man.

This is the male who is a product of an absent mama. Why has mama been absent? Any number of reasons. Classic cases include the mama who is subject to nervous problems or depression and is, to say the least, in need of rather frequent medication. Your basic swooner or victim of what they used to call the vapors. All of us in the South know the type. If you don't, just read Faulkner.

It's also possible that mama was highly repressed. She never fit the Melanie (nurturer) mold and yet she was forced into it by the traditions of Southern culture. She did what was expected of her and was never emotion-ally available to her son.

Or she may have died young, when our poor boy was yet a babe.

Then you have the wild-woman mama. This one didn't even pretend to do what was expected of her. She stayed drunk or gone or crazy or whatever and her little baby boy never did see enough of her.

There can be any number of reasons why mama neglected her boy. No doubt she loved him but she never did show it, or know how to show it. As a result, she produced Southern archetypal male Number Two: the Mama-Deprived. The one who is consistently attracted to women who are unattainable, just like mama. The following checklist will help you recognize him.

The Mama-Deprived Male

1. **Is more likely to have lived out of the South at one time or another.**

2. **Is likely to have accomplished, or be striving to accomplish, great things in the world to make up for the fact that his mother neglected him.**

3. **Thrives on ambiguity and the unexpected. Rarely appears or calls when he says he will; likes to play things by ear and make plans at the last minute.**

4. **Highly romantic when he chooses to be. Likes candlelit dinners, sends roses, drinks champagne. Knows his wines.**

5. **Has an elegant wardrobe; dresses and grooms well.**

6. **Has impeccable manners.**

7. **Typically has a highly developed sense of culture and good taste. Loves beautiful things— enjoys the ballet, symphony, and all things artistic.**

8. **Tends to be liberal in his political views. Shows great consideration to strangers but is less than generous with those close to him.**

9. **Needs a lot of time alone. May be a fly-fisherman, sculptor, musician, birdwatcher, or other solitary sensitive type. (Warning: Avoid writers and house painters.)**

10. **Has eclectic culinary tastes. Likes sushi and other exotic cuisine.**

Generally speaking, the Mama-Deprived Southern man has a tendency to appear caring and even loving on the surface due to his innate natural charm. Be warned—this man is often extremely self-involved, selfish, inconsiderate, and even downright mean when you scratch the surface. He will be a more difficult catch and, if you marry him, may take a lot of work before he is even in the trainable category of civilized domestic relations.

Chapter Five

THE DADDY FACTOR

*A*lthough the Mama Factor is the key to understanding and captivating your Southern man, the Daddy Factor plays its own role in your grasp of both his nature and yours.

The basic premise is twofold. One, Southern men tend to be just like their Daddies. If you want to know from whence your man came, where he's at, and where he's going, just take a look at his Daddy. If Daddy likes to sit in a duck blind all day, drink whiskey, and root for Florida State, so will your sweet Bubba. If Daddy is a salesman who's spent his life retailing cheap men's suits—Bubba will do likewise. He may sell cars or real estate instead of suits, but you get the idea.

If Daddy is a symphony conductor who has married and divorced three times and collects Wedgwood, Bubba probably at least plays in a band, is likely to be somewhat of a philanderer, and collects folk art.

The point of the first half of our Daddy Factor premise? To know your man (your prey) find out everything you can (discreetly) about his Daddy. You might argue that this goes against our earlier premise that Southern men are defined by the nature of their mother conflict, a.k.a. The Mama Factor. Not so. Just think about it—if your Bubba's Daddy married an unattainable woman, it's because he is the son of one. If Bubba's Daddy married a nurturer, it's because he is the son of one. And so on back into history for time immemorial, the matriarch has controlled the universe and all of society. Certainly all of Southern society. So let's put that argument to rest once and for all.

And let's move on to the second half of our premise: your own Daddy. Let's face it, when we Southern girls go looking for a mate, we tend to look for the characteristics we're so familiar with in our own Daddies. So take a long, well-considered look at your own Daddy and try to decide what you really love about him and what you could do without.

Do you love his loyalty and reliability but could do without his rigid insistence on certain routines and refusal to eat anything other than meat and potatoes? Then you want the basic Mama-Dependent man but toned down to a considerable degree. (We'll talk in the next chapter about toning down or gearing up to type.)

Do you admire the way your Daddy scorns the mushy and sentimental, knows everything about opera, looks great in a tux, and likes to frequent fancy restaurants? But you hate the fact that he has never told you he loves you and seems terrified of any kind of intimate conversation? Then your Daddy is a Mama-Deprived, for sure, and that's probably the type of man for you. But you want a Mama-Deprived who has had some feeling for others knocked into him somewhere along the way.

One warning: You must never, never expect that you will

be able to change your man. Bubba is as Bubba does. It has always been that way and always will be that way. That's why you must be sure you have set your sights on what you want before you apply *The Southern Rules* full strength.

You must admit, it would have been a disaster if Scarlett had actually ended up married to Ashley. He wasn't her type at all. And look at all the time she wasted on him.

And take the real Hillary. She's cut out for a Mama-Deprived, but she married the Mama-Dependent Bill. You can just see it written all over her face how impatient she is with him, how smothered she feels. Of course she met her own ambitious goals—maybe. Was it worth the sacrifice? Hmmm.

Chapter Six

FULLY
UNDERSTANDING
BUBBA

*A*t this point you should have an idea of whether you type as a Melanie, Zelda, or Hillary and whether the right man for you falls into the category of Mama-Dependent or Mama-Deprived. You have confirmed his tendencies and yours by checking out the Daddy Factor and are ready to refine your understanding of your darling future husband Bubba.

Remember, knowledge conquers all—a secret known by Southern women that somehow, over the ages, has managed to elude Southern men. This is as it should be. Too much knowledge confuses the Southern man and, when he is confused, he tends to run away. Which of course you don't want him to do.

Just in case you've been asleep for most of your life, trapped underground, or held hostage in a biosphere, the following checklist will help you further your understanding of your man by filling you in on some tendencies common to all Southern males.

Basic Bubba

1. In the South (like most places) men are terrified of women.

2. In the South (like most places), men will do anything for that first night of sex.

3. In the South (like most places), men don't talk to each other about their emotional involvement with the opposite sex.

4. In the South (like most places), men truly do want more than just a shallow relationship with no phone calls and lots of sex. They just think that's all they want.

5. In the South (like most places), men will expect you to take an interest in their hobbies and pursuits but will rarely take an interest in yours.

What are you supposed to do with this information now that you have it? It's all designed to help you manipulate Bubba to your ends. Get it? Let's take it point by point.

1. Men are terrified of women because they are afraid of power they don't understand. Fear is the simple reason why men don't call. It's why it is so hard for them to get around to asking you out in the first place. And it's why they are afraid to make a gesture such as sending flowers or a note or even a fresh possum steak. They are just plain scared little boys who aren't sure how you (the surrogate mama) will react. And of course, in a mama-dominated society, how mama reacts determines whether the sun will rise or not. Whether baby Bubba will live or die.

2. Where you have him is this: You are a potential sexual partner; his mama is not (or let's hope not). Thus the source of woman's power over man. He'll do anything for it so it only follows that to keep him doing anything, you need to withhold it for as long as possible. (More about this in Chapter Ten.)

3. You can safely assume that Bubba is not sitting at home or with his friends weaving elaborate schemes to "get" you the way that you are doing to get him. Bubba, I'm afraid to say, does not think in those terms. In fact he does not think at all about you. He may feel a want, a need, an attraction, but he does not analyze it, he does not pick it apart in slumber parties with his guy friends, he does not ask others for advice on how to captivate your heart, he does not even ask himself this stuff. He simply wants, he needs, he acts. Most important, he reacts—to you. So you must be very, very careful to always lead him on. Make sure he loves you more than you love him.

4. One thing Bubba does want that he may not know he wants is stability. A wife and a home are the one sure way to get that stability, especially in the South. Whether he's a Mama-Dependent or a Mama-Deprived, he needs someone to take care of him. I use that phrase very loosely. You must know that your success in catching your man, and your success in manipulating him after marriage, all will lie in the WAY you take care of him. You could, with a

Mama-Deprived, be taking care of your man without appearing to be doing anything at all.

5. Face the fact: Bubba will expect you to be as interested in the Auburn-Alabama game, the Talladega 500, or the Bass Masters Classic as he is. Face another fact: You're going to have to either be interested, pretend to be interested, or get interested. I strongly recommend not pretending. If you aren't already interested, get some reading material and start learning about his favorite hobby or pastime. This is a particularly useful strategy when it comes to beating out the competition.

The following two checklists will give you for some additional factors to help you fully identify and understand your ideal Mama-Dependent or Mama-Deprived Southern man.

Circumstances That Mediate the Mama Factor

1. **Number of children in his family and his position in the lineup.**

2. **If his mama was absent, whether there was a surrogate mama figure who raised him.**

3. **Whether he had sisters, how many, and their relative positions to him in the lineup.**

4. **If he was adopted.**

5. **If his daddy has passed away, how young Bubba was when it happened.**

WARNING: Things You Might Be Fooled into Thinking Mediate the Mama Factor but Don't

1. **Whether he has a college education or not.**

2. **His chosen job or profession.**

3. **Whether he's lived outside the South or not.**

4. **How well traveled he is generally.**

5. **His political views.**

6. **Whether he's been in therapy.**

7. **How macho he appears on the surface.**

8. **How smart he is.**

It's important that you listen real good here because you can be easily fooled by a man, especially a Southern man, into thinking the Mama Factor has been mediated or even alleviated by a long list of worldly factors. This is, as my dear old great Aunt Sally used to say, bull hockey.

The only thing that can tone down (or intensify) the Mama Factor are family circumstances that came into the picture long before you did. You can't do anything about them, so don't even try. If, after looking at his family makeup and fully understanding your Bubba, you decide he isn't right for you, have the courage to end the relationship and move on. You cannot change a man—especially a Southern man.

That said, let's take the mediating factors one by one.

1. The number of children in his family is critical. An only male child, be he Mama-Dependent or Mama-Deprived, will represent the strongest, most unmitigated specimen available of his type. In other words, if his mama was a smothering mama and he was her only child, look out. You got an extra-strength Mama-Dependent on your hands.

If his mama was an absent mama and he was her only child, look out. You got an extra-strength Mama-Deprived on your hands. Both, by the way, are the biggest kind of babies.

On the other hand, the more children there were in his family, the more mama's influence is mitigated. A Mama-Dependent type from a family of eight children is much more likely to be his own man, malleable and more mature, than a Mama-Dependent from a smaller family or an only-child family. Same thing goes for the Mama-Deprived types. Bottom line: If you fall between types, you want a man who falls between types. That kind of man is more likely to have come from a mama who gave him some siblings. So that, in other words, the poor fellow had a prayer of being socialized to some normal extent.

One word of caution here: If your man is from a large family but is the oldest or youngest, he may still suffer from the only-child syndrome because either way he could have spent a great deal of time either alone with mama or under her intense influence.

2. A surrogate mama can go a certain distance, sometimes a long way, in abrogating either the claustrophobic mama or the unavailable mama. In the South this was a benefit of the now nearly extinct domestic-servant system. It is not the purpose of this book to pass judgment either way on this system. But the fact remains that many Southern men now in their thirties and older had

a maid, be she black or white, who played a critical role in their upbringing. Not infrequently these domestic employees brought a certain breadth of worldview to the otherwise suffocatingly Mama-Dependent child's world; or, on the other side of the coin, taught the abjectly lonely Mama-Deprived child how to love. Naturally such surrogate-mother relationships are rarely so clear-cut. But you get the point. They can serve to mediate the Mama Factor.

Other surrogate mothering, to the same effect, may come from a live-in aunt, grandmother, or even an older sister (see next point).

3. If your Bubba had a sister or sisters, he is going to be to some extent more well-rounded than the only-child Mama-Dependent or Mama-Deprived or than the latter who comes from a family of brothers.

4. If Bubba was adopted, the Mama Factor and all other factors generally apply, especially if he was adopted as a baby. If he was adopted later than that, there's no telling.

5. If Bubba's daddy has passed, especially if he passed while Bubba was quite young, the Mama Factor will be strengthened. This also applies if his mama and daddy were divorced (with his mama retaining custody) while Bubba was young.

Chapter Seven

A FOOTNOTE ON AVOIDING THE NEW-AGE MALE

*G*irls, we'd all like to think that after x amount of therapy and x amount of time in the Peace Corps and x amount of time in search of root chakra, such cultural phenomena as the Mama Factor might fizzle out, lose their potency, and disappear from the human emotional and psychological landscape altogether.

Not so.

Don't make the mistake of thinking so. You will find yourself breaking the rules and losing your man before you can say "New Age."

I strongly counsel you to avoid the New-Age Male, especially the New-Age Southern Male, because he isn't real. He is someone pretending to be someone else. Is that the kind of person you want to spend the rest of your life with?

If your man doesn't know who he is and accept himself at this point, honey, you're lost and so is he.

To help you recognize the New-Age Male in the field and avoid him before you find yourself wasting your precious time on him, use the key identifiers in the checklist on the next page.

Field Guide to the New-Age Southern Male

1. Claims to have numerous female acquaintances who are "just friends."

2. Actively pursues a religion originating in the Far East.

3. May be a member of a country-dance society.

4. Wears Birkenstocks.

5. Buys food at health-food stores.

6. Listens to self-help tapes.

7. Is in, or has been in, therapy. (If he actually is a therapist, avoid him at all costs!)

8. May be a member of an old-time or bluegrass music band.

9. Devotes inordinate number of hours to community service work.

10. Does not have a job that pays very well.

11. Purports that sex is just a natural form of communication between animals and that we are, after all, animals.

12. Claims to feel more comfortable with women than with men.

This guy is just plain more trouble than he's worth. Because you are Scarlett, the Queen of the South, you deserve the Rhett of your dreams. A real man! Not some bum in sandals. Do yourself a favor and don't even think about investing your valuable time in this pretender. Once you get through all the smoke and mirrors, you're just going to have to deal with the Mama Factor anyway. Might as well start right off there to begin with.

Chapter Eight

STRATEGIZING FOR THE MAMA FACTOR

*Y*our basic strategy is simple. You must, more or less, replicate his mama.

If your man is a Mama-Dependent, you want to play up your homemaking skills. If he is Mama-Deprived, you want to—well, basically reject him as much as you can without actually chasing him away.

Remember that you must do all this within the basic context of playing hard-to-get. Just because your man is Mama-Dependent doesn't mean you should chase after him with a pot of chicken soup and a fresh-baked apple pie. No— you just want to casually have these things around, and have them be fabulous, when he comes over for dinner.

By the same token, just because your man is Mama-Deprived doesn't mean you can't give him little gifts or make suggestions that will help him. Just do it in a very unsentimental way, and do it infrequently—after he's done something for you first.

Following are some basic pointers. Keep them handy!

How to Captivate Mama-Dependent Bubba

1. Don't forget, first and foremost, you are Scarlett and he is just someone to eat barbecue with. You lived without other men and you can live without him.

2. If he is Mama-Dependent, he will be dazzled by proficient domestic skills. However you must display them casually, as if he just happens to be in the right place at the right time to discover this about you.

3. Always have some delicious homemade snacks on hand, just in case.

4. A delicious home-cooked dinner will go a long way, but don't push this too hard too soon. Let it take place in its own good time, no sooner than the third date.

5. If he leaves items of clothing at your house (don't encourage this, but if it happens) return them promptly, washed and pressed.

6. If he offers an opportunity to meet his family, accept graciously and behave graciously.

7. When the opportunity arises, take him on a sumptuous picnic (prepared by you of course).

8. When you are at his place, always clean up tidily after yourself and leave the place a little subtly cleaner overall then when you arrived.

9. Make an effort to get along well with his pets (which, if he is Mama-Dependent, he is likely to have).

10. As the opportunity arises, curry favor with his parents and siblings by doing and making nice little things for them.

How to Captivate Mama-Deprived Bubba

1. Always remember, first and foremost, you are Scarlett and he is just someone to eat barbecue with. You lived without other men and you can live without him.

2. If he is Mama-Deprived, he will be frightened by domesticity. It is something unfamiliar that he doesn't know how to deal with—so he will run. Display as little overt domesticity as possible—although you want your home to evidence all the charm and character that you embody. When he asks, however, about particular objects of art or decor in your home, you can be casually informative.

3. You want to be as unavailable as possible to this man, without leading him to think you are uninterested. Be warm and cordial but SO very busy (doing things that are NOT nurturing-related).

4. NEVER call him.

5. Never cook for him. If you eat at your place, order out.

6. If you have dinner together, a restaurant is the best suggestion. Don't suggest your place or his unless he does. Let him pay.

7. If he offers an opportunity to meet members of his family, find a way to politely but credibly beg off or postpone this occurrence.

8. Never independently contact members of his family or try to get close to him through his family. A card at Christmas is enough, at most.

9. He will probably not have pets. If he does, they will be cats. Ignore them.

10. Don't drop hints about gifts you'd like for your birthday, Valentine's Day, or Christmas. Be silent. If he gives you something, accept it with a casual "Thank you. But I feel so bad—I didn't get anything for you."

In general, as they say in fly-fishing, you want to "match the hatch." That is, you want to duplicate as closely as possible the Mama Factor—the originating female-male relationship that formed his whole attitude toward life.

When you're first getting to know him, the safest route is to assume he is Mama-Deprived. You can't go wrong by remaining too aloof at first. But try to figure out quickly which category he is truly in so you can adjust your behavior accordingly. With the Mama-Deprived, you'll want to remain aloof. With the Mama-Dependent, you'll want to warm up a little based on how dependent he is. Be forewarned that with the Mama-Dependent, you do risk the possibility of losing him if you play it too cool—he might think you really aren't interested.

One final word of caution: When I say "warm up" I mean it always within the context of the Scarlett Checklist. That is, never chase a man. That sort of thing is pure-dee beneath you. It will instantly kill the mystery and Bubba will be gone. You always want to "warm up" or "cool off" toward Bubba within the context of remaining just out of arm's reach. That tantalizing "so near and yet so far" taste of your presence is how you want to handle him for the rest of your life. It is, quite simply, the secret to generations of female manipulation of males. The rock of our civilization. Never abandon it—unless you want him to abandon you.

Chapter Nine

THE FIRST DATE: MAGNOLIAS AND MOONLIGHT

That first date should be a magical event if he is the man for you. When you look back on it, there should be sparkles all around it. You should float home on a cloud, and everyone who looks at you will be able to see the glow.

It doesn't always happen this way. But you can help ensure it will be that way when it needs to be—that is, when the man is right and you want to be sure you see him again.

It's so easy it's almost embarrassing to have to write it down. But for the sake of future generations who have never heard of a Southern belle or seen a Tallulah Bankhead movie, here's how it's done.

First-Date Tips

1. **Buy something new to wear. You may have something perfectly good in your closet, but something new will make you feel special.**

2. **Wear a dress.**

3. **To whatever extent the date is subtly within your power, encourage it to take place over dinner in a nice restaurant where you can bring**

to bear the full power of your hair, makeup, and wardrobe (vs. a hiking expedition or day of fishing).

4. Wear scent.

5. If you are meeting him (which you should do), be at least 15 minutes late.

6. Arrange to have a friend call you at the restaurant in the middle of the evening. When you come back to the table after taking the call, apologize for the interruption but remain mysterious about the nature of the call as well as the caller.

7. Be a good listener. There is nothing a man likes so well as talking about himself.

8. Don't drink too much. No one is attracted to a sloppy woman.

9. Eat like a bird.

10. Laugh at his humor, even if he doesn't have any. But don't laugh too much, too loud, or too long. Keep the conversation light and breezy.

11. If he is Mama-Dependent, compliment him on something he is wearing. If he is Mama-Deprived, make no reference to his appearance.

12. Be the first one to initiate the termination of the date.

13. If he drives you home, don't let him come in.

14. Don't kiss him except in a friendly manner, on the cheek.

15. Don't ask him to call you. If he asks if he can call you again, agree politely, but make sure you're busy and can't come to the phone when he does call (make him call at least twice).

16. Never forget how fortunate this man is that you have agreed to grace his life with your charming company.

Chapter Ten

KEEP SEX
OUT OF IT
(DON'T WASTE
AMMUNITION)

*M*any of you are not going to like this part of *The Southern Rules* but I have to be very forceful in telling you that this is the heart of the matter.

How do you think Southern women have controlled their men from time immemorial? The judicious granting of one's physical affections is not to be taken lightly and is a rule not to be violated if you hope to capture your man and keep him.

The single most important *Southern Rule* is that you absolutely should not have sex with a man until you are engaged to him.

Sorry, I know you don't like it—but it is critical. Respect is critical to every successful relationship. So is the reward system.

He won't respect you if you give him sex too soon. And you won't have any way left of controlling or inducing the behavior you want if you've taken away his incentive.

There you have it: Control yourself. Do whatever you have to do. But don't let him have any. If that chases him away, he was not the man for you. He will never love or respect you anyway, so you've lost nothing.

You'll also find, if you haven't already, that in a romantic relationship sex changes everything. Not necessarily for the man, but for the woman. Bubba will still go along being the same old Bubba whether he gets you into bed or not. He certainly won't think any more of you by getting you into bed, you can be sure of that.

But the moment you have gone to bed with him, you'll start thinking differently of him. Your thinking will get fuzzy. You stand a very good chance of acting needy and sentimental. You'll have a hard time analyzing the situation clearly, doing the right thing, and drawing the necessary boundaries. Next thing you know you've broken *The Southern Rules* and chased him away.

Take my word for it and protect yourself! Don't let Bubba, no matter how great you think he is, take away your sense of yourself. Keep your sacred font holy until Bubba has proved himself worthy and presented you with a ring.

Ten Things to Do Instead of Having Sex

1. **Eat something rich and sweet, like fried pie or Goo-Goo Clusters.**

2. **Distract him by turning on ESPN.**

3. **Ask him to tell you again about his truck (or boat or car).**

4. **Get him to show you the tricks his dog does.**

5. Suddenly remember you have to pick up your laundry at your mama's before she goes to sleep, or you won't have a thing to wear tomorrow.

6. Tell him you have to get home to let your dog/cat out.

7. Tell him you need your beauty sleep and it's time for him to leave.

8. Go see a late movie.

9. Go for a walk.

10. If you get absolutely positively desperate, tell him this is an inopportune time of the month (but remember—good Southern girls avoid discussing their menses).

Chapter Eleven

MORE TOOLS
FOR TAMING
THE BEAST

*H*ere are twenty-five miscellaneous tips to help you snag him good.

1. **Slap him (then well up into tears and apologize).**

2. **Let him see lingerie in your house (i.e. hanging up to dry in the bathroom) but don't let him see it on you.**

3. **Show a little cleavage every once in a while, on a special or dressy occasion. (Don't show it during the workday.)**

4. **Leave a list lying out with men's names and phone numbers written in your handwriting.**

5. **Send yourself roses at a time when you know he'll be coming over to your place or your office.**

6. **Keep a bottle of champagne (or a six-pack, depending on your man) chilled in your refrigerator.**

7. Leave an empty jeweler's box in plain sight.

8. At all times, keep your grooming impeccable (be prepared for the unexpected).

9. Be late arriving and early leaving.

10. On dress-up occasions, wear spike heels. (Again, never during the workday or you'll just look cheap.)

11. Take a trip to an exotic place by yourself.

12. Don't tell who you went on the trip with or didn't go on the trip with.

13. Make sure your home always smells good (i.e. good food cooking, perfumy clean smells in the bathroom).

14. Don't overuse intoxicants. If you must, never do so in his presence.

15. Avoid sentimentality in what you say.

16. Never express verbally any need, no matter how mild, to see him.

17. Get in candlelight as much as possible.

18. Don't go around telling people you're seeing Bubba. Let him be the one to do that.

19. In general, dress in conservative classy clothes that show your figure to its best advantage. Don't wear fluffy, froufrou, fake country-western, or earth-mother-peasant, even if that's the way his mama dresses. Men are formed by the way their mothers treated them, not by how their mothers look.

20. Never discuss with him the other men you date or have dated. It is much more intriguing to be mysterious.

21. Insult him once in a while.

22. Do not cuss. This frightens and unsettles Bubba. He does, for the most part, want a feminine female.

23. Learn to shoot. An attractive woman competently wielding a firearm is a major turn-on for Bubba.

24. Learn first aid. Another Bubba fantasy: being field-dressed by Florence Nightingale.

25. Paint your toenails.

Chapter Twelve

MEETING
HIS FAMILY

$\mathcal{M}$eeting his family is not something you want to think a lot about in advance—if you think too much about it, you'll be too nervous. You'll forget how to act and you might blow it. Plus you'll be so busy worrying about the way you appear to them that you'll neglect your own important work, which can only take place on this important occasion.

And that is: Get a good close look, firsthand, at the Mama who made Bubba what he is today. Not to mention the Daddy and sisters and brothers.

You'll need this information, especially for effective Bubba management after marriage and beyond. Watch the way Bubba relates to his mama and the way his mama and daddy interact. This is what you can expect for you and Bubba.

Make note of any information Mama imparts as to Bubba's likes and dislikes, favorite foods, etc. If she's a big-mouth, as many Southern boys' mamas are, she'll be likely to let slip some info about your rivals, either past or present. This is always useful because you can use it to go after them and quash them for good. (In a subtle and ladylike way, of course.)

The important thing to remember is to be yourself, don't speak unless spoken to, act in a gracious and ladylike manner, and absorb information!

Use the following tips for a successful first meeting with Bubba's family.

Tips for Your First Family Visit

1. **Don't push for this event to happen! It will happen in its own good time.**

2. **Don't bring a gift the first time.**

3. **Do write a thank-you note afterward if a meal was served.**

4. **Don't talk too much! Keep your mouth shut unless spoken to.**

5. **If questions about your romantic past are asked, be vague.**

6. **It goes without saying, but we'll say it anyway, look your very best. This is another little trick for driving Bubba wild. You want to look so good he can't take his eyes off you—and he'll be further enchanted by the fact that, in front of his family, he can't touch you. Don't be surprised, in fact, if he tries to jump you afterward (but don't let him).**

7. **Keep a close eye on your manners and make sure they are impeccable.**

8. Listen to what others have to say and ask questions that require them to open up and talk about themselves.

9. Closely observe the family interaction. This is what you'll have on your hands if you marry Bubba.

10. Closely observe the individuals themselves. This is a good opportunity for you to decide whether you can live with these people or not. You surely will be stuck with them, after all, when and if you marry Bubba.

11. If they hint or ask you outright about your future plans or any future plans you might have with Bubba, be vague. If you've been married before, be particularly vague about this fact.

12. If any of the females, Mama in particular, sends any veiled jabs your way, simply smile sweetly.

13. Shake their hands when you are introduced to family members, and again upon leaving. It is permissible to give Mama a token hug and an air-kiss.

14. Do not discuss politics or religion. Be prepared to discuss football and cooking.

15. A final note on wardrobe. Count on it, you will be scored heavily on how you look. And you DO want to look fabulous, but by all means do not dress in a flashy or revealing manner. Be sure your clothes are modest and in good taste and that you have on sensible shoes in good condition. Bubba's mama is sure to check out your shoes and also will draw conclusions based on whether your jewelry is cheap and flashy or quiet and tasteful.

Chapter Thirteen

MURDER:
HOW SOUTHERN
WOMEN DEAL
WITH REJECTION

Not every man is right for every woman and thus we go through the world casting each other aside until we make that perfect match. We girls would all like to think that we are always in the position of being the rejecter, not the rejectee, but let's face it. No one gets out of life without having her heart broken at least one time.

Yankee women may retire to their rooms and weep their lives away when they are rejected, but not us Southerners. Oh no. For us, revenge is a way of life. We live and breathe it. The South was built on revenge and that's a fact that ain't going to change anytime soon. So when Bubba rejects you, by all means—SEEK REVENGE!

If you know some fullbacks or maybe someone your brother works with who can take him out into a dark alley and do a number on him ...

Now, now, I was only joking. This man has taken a big enough chunk of your soul as it is, you don't want to get tangled up even further on the dark side.

What I mean by seeking revenge is something along the lines of that cliché "Living well is the best revenge."

If you've been rejected, go straight back to your Scarlett

Checklist and remind yourself that, while women are all-purpose creatures, men have a limited range of use in this world and that's all well and good but it is NOT worth wasting away over. There are plenty of men available to eat barbecue with you, Scarlett. So go out there right away and get yourself into even better physical shape, even more gorgeous looks, some new clothing and get right back out there in the world and eat barbecue.

Your revenge will come, I promise. It will come when that idiotic Bubba who rejected you sees you all aglow on the arm of another man. When he hears that you are engaged to someone far better and more deserving than he. And when he runs into you in a few years at that class reunion or Christmas party and sees what a knockout you still are, even after two kids. He'll see how adoringly your husband gazes at you, as do all the other men in the room, and he'll kick himself with regret for letting you get away.

That, my dear Scarlett, is even better than murder. It is the sweetest revenge we ever get in this life.

So wipe your tears and get your flirtatious rear end in gear. The following ten hints will help you regain control.

Scarlett's Revenge

1. **Allow yourself to cry for twenty minutes at the very most. Any more than that he doesn't deserve, and it will make your eyes puffy and unsightly. He doesn't deserve to do that to you either.**

2. If it helps you feel better, stick pins in his picture or doodle on it so he looks ridiculous. You may keep this harmless voodoo in sight for a few days just to remind yourself of what an idiot he is, but put it away after that because even stuck full of pins and with horns on his head, he doesn't merit that much of your attention.

3. Burn something significantly symbolic of him.

4. Allow yourself a few drinks if this helps ease the pain and helps you sleep better at night.

5. Pamper yourself to the absolute ultimate: Take long deliciously scented baths, light candles, get a massage and facial, buy yourself something new to wear.

6. Take extra-good care of your health. Get eight hours of sleep at night, get plenty of exercise, eat a balanced diet, and take your vitamins.

7. Absolutely do not under any circumstances call him.

8. Do not write him notes or try to get to him through his mama or the rest of his family or friends.

9. It is acceptable to appear at social functions you know he will also be attending as long as you are sure you are fully in control of yourself and can act breezy and blasé about running into him. Be sure you are looking fabulous and have a good-looking date.

10. Prime a well-placed girlfriend or two to drop comments around him regarding how great you are doing, how wonderful you are looking, and how happy you are.

Chapter Fourteen

THE BUDDY
FACTOR

Friends mean a lot to your darling Bubba. The stupefying, unmitigated silence of buddies silently fishing the same stream, mutely munching down piles of potato chips while they take in a ball game on TV, the hoisting of a cool one over the usual slaps on the back, complaints about work, and occasional dirty joke are all a mysteriously important, and to Bubba and his buddies, an endlessly fascinating fixture of Southern male culture.

Whether your man is a Mama-Dependent or Mama-Deprived, he will now and always require a certain amount of time off with his buddies doing basically nothing. The role of we females is not to understand this mystery, but to accept it. For Bubba it is not the doing of nothing that is significant but the fact of just being there. Call it male bonding if you will, although I dislike that New-Age term. There is something going on here far deeper and more elemental than a male-sensitivity session. In fact it might be more accurate to call it a male-insensitivity session.

Whatever you want to call it, the more accepting you are (on the surface), the better your chances of landing Bubba and keeping him. You have your own ways of encouraging him to spend time with you rather than his buddies.

Use the following ten tips for coping with the Buddy Factor.

Coping with Bubba's Buddies

1. **Never complain or argue when Bubba has something to do with his friends.**

2. **Act as if you're glad he's going off on his own.**

3. **Tell him it will be good for him.**

4. **Don't ask him what time he'll get home.**

5. **The next day or anytime afterward, don't ask him about his male get-together. Act like you don't care.**

6. **Never ask to go with him.**

7. **If he invites you to go, decline.**

8. **If his preferred scenario for buddy time is anything that does not involve drinking or hanging out in bars (like building model cars or playing par-3 golf), by all means encourage it as much as you can. Once you are married you will want him out of the house and he will need a harmless hobby.**

9. If you haven't already, cultivate your own outside interests that require you to go off from time to time with your own female buddies.

10. If he needs three or more nights out with his buddies a week—especially if the nights out revolve around drinking and bars—drop him.

Chapter Fifteen

THE FOOTBALL FACTOR

*Y*ou can't get away from sports in the South. Chances are good, especially if your Bubba is Mama-Dependent, that he is a football fan. Even if he is Mama-Deprived, or anywhere in between, he will no doubt be obsessed with some sport. He may be consumed by fishing, or golf, or bowling— or any combination of one or more sports.

Your tendency may be to see his chosen sport as your rival. Do not make this mistake. His sport is your friend. Especially in the long term, when you will see that Bubba needs something to keep him occupied and out of trouble (see Chapter Fourteen, "The Buddy Factor"). Sports is the ideal way for Bubba to occupy himself and stay out of trouble. By trouble, I mean drinking and women—the kind of women who hang around bars.

While you want your Bubba to have his time with the guys, you will also want to be able to participate, at least to the extent of conversing, in his sport. Don't get me wrong. I am not by any stretch suggesting you become one of the guys. Quite the contrary. I am suggesting that if you don't know anything about his favored sport, learn something and begin to take an interest. I say this for several reasons.

One, you'll need common ground if you're going to snag Bubba and you can't expect him to take an interest in your hobbies.

Two, men tend to admire women who can intelligently discuss a sport, provided they aren't know-it-alls who threaten Bubba's masculinity.

Three, it will give you something to talk about with his family. No doubt Bubba's particular sporting interests are shared by his kinfolk. This is especially likely in regard to football and other team loyalties.

Four, it will give you an edge over other females.

The following are some other important pointers.

Applied Football Science (and Other Sports-Related Tips)

1. **Find out which college football team he supports before you reveal or proclaim any biases of your own. You will have an instant advantage if you both root for the Tigers (or whatever).**

2. **Learn all you can about the team he supports so you can discuss it with him.**

3. **Find out what team(s) his family supports.**

4. **Draw the line at getting so enthusiastic that you compete with his buddies for the position of**

football soulmate. This is sacred territory and you don't want to violate it because you would risk coming between him and his friends. That can cause big problems.

5. If he has an entire room in his house dedicated to Bear Bryant or some other sports icon, drop him—unless you are equally obsessed with the same demigod. If that is the case, marry him.

6. If he and a few friends get together an impromptu game of touch football and he invites you to participate, decline.

7. If he and a few buddies are getting together to watch the game, either in a public place or one of the guys' houses, and you are invited to participate, decline.

8. If he asks you to go with him to a football game, go. Be sure to wear a fabulous outfit and get your hair done that day. But don't get overdressed, i.e. in a mink coat, catsuit, or metallic leather.

9. If he shows up to pick you up for the game with his face painted or wearing a wig in the team colors, stop dating him.

10. If he gets so violently stressed out during the course of the game or is so bent out of shape afterward that he scares you, stop dating him.

11. If he enjoys the game to a sensible degree, does not wear anything outlandish, accepts the outcome of the game for what it is, appears willing to get on with life without ranting and raving, and invites you to a lovely dinner after the game during which he doesn't even bring up the subject of football, marry him.

12. There are sports in the world besides football although many of us in the South do not know this fact. Because sports are so essential to life in the South, you should have at least one sport of your own. Golf and tennis are excellent all-purpose social tools. Billiards is a very sexy game for a woman to excel at. Every Southern woman should know how to shoot a gun. Bowling is fun to do with your girlfriends and a great way to meet down-to-earth blue-collar types. Pick the sport that fits your interests, goals, and aspirations. And if you really want to turn Bubba on, get very very good at it.

Chapter Sixteen

THE FOOD
FACTOR

$\mathcal{I}$f you are a well-brought up Southern female you should not even have to read this chapter. However, for the sake of completing our gospel on dating and mating in the South, we must not skip over the Food Factor.

Whoever first said that the way to a man's heart is through his stomach should have contracted to get a royalty on that statement. Whether you do a good job picking out just the right restaurant or prepare a meal calculated to satisfy all his senses, the food you share with Bubba will influence his heart.

If he's a Mama-Dependent and his mother was a wonderful cook, you better sharpen your kitchen tools and get out your favorite recipes. Cooking well will absolutely be required if you are to catch and keep your Bubba. If he is Mama-Dependent and his mother was not a great cook, you're in an excellent position. This will be like shooting fish in a barrel.

If he's Mama-Deprived, especially to the extreme degree, be careful. You don't want to rush the nurturing. A home-cooked meal, no matter how fabulous, could scare him right out of your life. In fact, a home-cooked meal served too early in the relationship, especially if it IS fabulous, is almost guaranteed to scare him away. So go slowly with the Mama-Deprived Bubba. You want him to know you share his discriminating palate when it comes to fine food and wine, but let it happen all in good time. Let him take the lead.

The following are some tips on applying the Food Factor. Be sure you adjust your timing and strength of application to the level of Mama-Dependency or Mama-Deprivation of your man.

Feeding the Hungry Bubba

1. **You don't have to be able to cook everything well. Just be sure you can cook a few things extraordinarily well.**

2. **Draw up four or five basic menus that fit a variety of occasions and keep practicing them until you've mastered them.**

3. **Find out what dishes are Bubba's favorites.**

4. **Find out what his food dislikes are.**

5. **Keep some snacks or hors d'oeuvres around that suit his culinary personality. Mama-Dependents tend to like the basic stuff, i.e. cookies, chips, and dip; Mama-Depriveds tend to like the more esoteric items, i.e. smoked salmon, brie, and grapes.**

6. Develop some skills in field-dressing game, even if it's just the know-how to clean a fish. The South was built on the backbone of women who could clean and cook wild game and Southern men have an admiration for this trait built into their subconscious.

7. You must know how to make good corn bread.

8. The first time you have him over for dinner, make something you can prepare to a large extent ahead of time. You want the preparation to look breezy and effortless. The last thing you want is to have him come in and find you sweating over a hot stove.

9. Consider the season and prepare your meal accordingly. You don't want to serve something like chili that will make him sweat in summer. Work toward an overall gratifying sensory experience.

10. Don't ever offer to cook for him at his house. You won't know where things are, and you may blow it. It's hard to control outcomes—and appearances—when cooking at someone else's house.

Chapter Seventeen

THE IMPORTANCE
OF CHURCH

The role of church in Southern life must not be underestimated. Do not make the mistake of thinking that because Bubba does not go to church or talk much about church that church is not important.

If nothing else, church will be important after you have children. For this reason, it is a time-tested tenet of the Southern code that a woman marry a man from not only the same religion but the same denomination as she: Baptists marry Baptists, Methodists marry Methodists, Presbyterians marry Presbyterians. Nowadays it is not so critical that you marry exactly your denomination, but it is recommended that you marry into the same faith and that you and Bubba have similar religious beliefs.

If he doesn't believe in God and you do, there's going to be trouble down the road, and I suggest you stop dating him.

If you have given your life to Jesus and he's exploring Krishna, I suggest you do not try to save him.

If you are Catholic and he is Jewish, I suggest you call it off before it goes any further.

Don't get me wrong—I am not denying that love has the power to conquer all and there are many examples out there of successful mixed-religion couples. I do not judge them and you shouldn't either. But I am here to tell you that married life is hard enough without adding that obstacle to your list of challenges.

I'm here to tell you what *The Southern Rules* are. I didn't make them—they just are. And in the South, mixing religions is against the rules.

There are many other reasons why church is important in your dating and married life.

First, there are few places better than church to meet eligible single men.

Second, if you and Bubba share similar religious beliefs, going to church together can be a powerful growth experience for you as individuals and as a couple.

Third, you're much more likely to get along with his family if you share beliefs.

Fourth, after you're married, church provides a wonderfully healthy social environment you can both indulge in. It provides peer pressure that your Bubba may need to stay on the beam (without you having to play the role of bad cop). And it gives Bubba some safe buddies to hang around with—the types who will reinforce, rather than tear down, his role in your home and family.

Following are some reasons to make church part of dating Bubba.

Go to Church and Get Your Reward

1. There are few better venues for meeting decent eligible men.

2. A church social is a great place to show off your cooking skills.

3. Join him at church for a social activity and you won't have to worry about drawing sexual boundaries—they're drawn for you.

4. You can relax and be yourself when you see him at church because you know you're in a safe environment.

5. You'll probably already know enough about him before the first date so that your chances of success down the road are greater.

6. You may also have an opportunity to meet members of his family in the church setting. If you like them, so much the better. If you spot trouble, you never have to date him at all and will have avoided all that heartache.

7. If you didn't meet the Bubba of Your Dreams at church, take him to church with you. If he's reluctant to go, drop him.

8. If you take Bubba to church with you and he handles himself well, being polite and making conversation with a variety of types of people, this is a good sign. You might want to marry him.

9. If the two of you decide to get married, do it in a church. The vows will be more significant and church will give you a solid grounding for your future family—even if you never have children.

10. After you're married, church provides a solid guardrail to keep you both on the beam. There will be safe friends and good role models for Bubba and the same for you—not to mention your children.

Chapter Eighteen

THE IMPORTANCE OF TEARS

This will be a short chapter because there are only a few instances in which you will ever need to use tears as a strategic strike weapon.

Please keep in mind that, for the most part, Bubba is confused and disturbed by your tears. And, need I say it again, you don't want to confuse Bubba because when he's confused he gets scared and runs away.

So for the most part, keep your crying to yourself. Except:

1. **After you have done something terribly wrong and want him to know how contrite you are.**

2. **At the funeral of one of his close friends or family members (provided you knew this person).**

3. **At very sad movies (but pretend you aren't crying). This will demonstrate what a feminine, sensitive little thing you are and make him feel tender and protective toward you.**

4. **When you really, really want him to do something with you or for you and have no other way to get him to do it. He'll do it just to stop your crying. (Warning: Use this tactic only after marriage. Before marriage it might scare him away.)**

5. **When something is bad wrong and you don't know how else to bring up the subject. Tears will guarantee that he will ask with alarm: What's wrong? (Again, this is a tactic best reserved for after marriage.)**

Contrary to popular opinion, you should NOT cry when he tells you for the first time that he loves you, when he presents you with The Ring, when he hurts your feelings, when you are trying to get him to buy you something, or any time within three days of an event that requires you to look your absolute best.

Chapter Nineteen

THE WEDDING

*W*e all know that weddings are not for men. They are for women. Especially in the South. They are for women and their mamas. The men might as well just step aside and get out of the way until it's all over because this event does not concern them, their opinions are not wanted, and they are at best a sidebar to the whole show.

However, if you want a successful marriage, it is a good idea to get off on the right foot by offering Bubba token participation in his own wedding. True, all that is really required of him is to show up. But part of your goal as his future wife is to make him feel important. So start now. Let him voice a few (small) preferences and let him make a few (small) decisions that will allow him to point with pride at your wedding album and show his buddies that he was actually part of this event—or so he will think. What could it hurt to let him nurse that little fantasy?

That said, let's make sure we understand the inviolable *Southern Rules* that apply to the successful wedding.

The Southern Wedding Rules

1. Make sure you get an engagement ring. An engagement without a ring is not an engagement.

2. Don't let him pick out the engagement ring. This is something you should at least have discussed or hinted at so he knows what kind of ring you want.

3. The one decision you need to reserve exclusively for yourself is the dress. Don't let anyone influence you otherwise. You'll have a hard enough time keeping control of this day; you can at least be the one who makes the final decision on the dress.

4. You can let him decide things like whether or not to have a groom's cake, whom to invite from among his friends, and what he will wear.

5. You can let him have input into other decisions such as where the reception will be held, what kind of music will be played, and what the invitation should look like. (But he doesn't necessarily have to make the decision.)

6. While you might argue with your own mother about certain details and decisions, try not to disagree with his mother. Let her just have her way.

7. If your mama and his mama want to fight it out, that's their problem.

8. Do have the wedding in a church or at least have the service conducted by a minister.

9. Go over your vows in advance. Try to combine this with a pleasurable experience like a nice dinner as it is a chore he will be a little afraid of.

10. If there's to be drinking at the reception, make sure you have final say over which of his friends will be invited.

11. Try not to cry, it will mess up your makeup and you'll look bad afterward in the wedding pictures.

12. You'd better hope, if you don't know by now, that Bubba can dance.

13. Don't insist on approval of the bachelor party venue and agenda. He needs to know he's not on a leash (yet). Besides, if you give him free rein he's liable to do something perfectly tame. If you worry out loud too much about that evening, you might as well drive him to the strip joint yourself.

14. If he gets a case of cold feet at the last minute, don't panic. And don't try to force the issue. Go back to The Southern Rules and ask him lightly if maybe it wouldn't be better if you just called the whole thing off. Above all, this is not the time to cry.

15. Don't get drunk at your own reception.

Chapter Twenty

THE IRON HAND IN THE VELVET GLOVE: TIPS FOR LIFETIME CONTROL OF YOUR MAN

1. Never forget that sex is the greatest incentive in the world.

2. Never let down on your looks no matter how old you are or how long you've been married.

3. Never overtly control; induce instead.

4. Never underestimate the power of a great home-cooked meal.

5. Never come between your Bubba and his friends.

6. Never come between your Bubba and his mama.

7. Do come between your Bubba and dangerous other women, but do it subtly by looking better, being a better conversationalist, and flirting with other men.

8. Never underestimate the power of jealousy. All he has to do is see you flirting once and he will toe the line.

9. If you see him flirting, pretend you are unaware of it or don't care.

10. Don't beg or manipulate him into buying you things. Let him buy you things on his own.

11. Brag about him when you are out with other couples.

12. Do NOT brag about him to your single girlfriends.

13. Encourage him to pursue hobbies and outside interests. When he announces he has been invited on a fishing trip, be enthusiastic.

14. Develop outside interests and hobbies of your own.

15. Get very proficient in at least one sport.

16. Take care of him. If he's Mama-Dependent, this means nurture him. If he's Mama-Deprived, this means leave him alone.

17. Surprise him from time to time.

18. Make him worry about you once in awhile.

19. Do things that will gain you recognition in the community and make him proud to be with such an important and respected woman. But be very humble about your accomplishments.

20. Go to church.

21. Keep a nice home.

22. Let him have his own Bubba-spot in your home, and let him keep it however he wants to.

23. Don't paint your house pink, it will humiliate him.

24. Don't fight over money. Decide in advance whether you are going to keep your money together or separate. (But even if you decide to keep it together, keep a secret stash for yourself.)

25. Don't let him get fat. But if he does get fat, don't try to make him lose weight—he'll do it when he's ready.

26. If he smokes, let him have a smoking area either in or outside the house.

27. If you can afford it, you should each have your own TV.

28. If you can afford it, you should each have your own car.

29. Don't ever insist that he call you when he's away from home.

30. Don't give him grief when he comes in late. Do things that will make him always want to be on time.

31. Remember, even after you're married, that you are and will always be Scarlett—the most tantalizing girl at the barbecue. Even the original Scarlett forgot that and allowed herself to become, for a moment, a mush-mouthed blubbering fool—not the fiery charmer that Rhett married. Take a lesson from Scarlett: Don't ever forget The Southern Rules.

Chapter Twenty-One

THE SOUTHERN RULES
IN A NUTSHELL

1. **Remember Scarlett and Keep Her Holy.**

2. **Know Your Prey (and Yourself).**

3. **Understand the Mama Factor.**

4. **Understand the Daddy Factor.**

5. **Avoid the New-Age Male.**

6. **Strategize for the Mama Factor.**

7. **Keep Sex Out of It.**

8. **Make Sure He Loves You More Than You Love Him.**

9. **Play It Cool and Charming with His Family.**

10. **Flirting Well Is the Best Revenge.**

11. **Let Him Have His Buddies.**

12. **Factor in Football.**

13. **Feed Him Well.**

14. **Go to Church.**

15. **Use Tears Sparingly and Strategically.**

16. **Let Him Have Token Input into the Wedding.**

17. **For Lifetime Control, Don't Manipulate—Induce.**

ELLEN PATRICK is the author of *Help! I'm Southern and I Can't Stop Eating!*, *The Cowgirl's Guide to Love*, and *Aunt Sally's Cornpone Remedies and Claptrap Cures* (Crane Hill Publishers). She has also authored four children's books: *The Magic Easter Egg, The Very Little Duck, A Bunny's Tale*, and *Three Baby Chicks* (Simon & Schuster). Under the name E. J. Sullivan, she is the author of *The Redneck Night Before Christmas* and *A Redneck Christmas Carol* (Sweetwater Press).

Ellen Patrick maintains firm control over her very own Bubba, deep in the heart of Alabama.